The Christmas Story
Calligraphy by
Carol J. Haile
Paintings by
Freiman F. Stoltzfus

The Christmas Story

From the Gospels according to St. Matthew and St. Luke

Calligraphy by Carol J. Haile
Paintings by Freiman F. Stoltzfus

Book design by Carol J. Haile and Freiman F. Stoltzfus

FIRST EDITION

Library of Congress Control Number: 2001092655

P.O. Box 6892
Wyomissing, PA 19610-0892
USA

ISBN 0-9711236-0-8

Summary: A book for young and old alike, this is a retelling of the first Christmas. Using words taken directly from the Gospels according to St. Matthew & St. Luke, the book is set in the farmlands of the Amish community. The story is told in fraktur, the script of the early Pennsylvania Germans, and illustrated with scenes from everyday Amish life.

Printed and bound in Pennsylvania, USA

To my grandmother ~

M. Florence R. Drace Spielman

~ Carol

To my mother ~

Susan Fisher Stoltzfus

~ Freiman

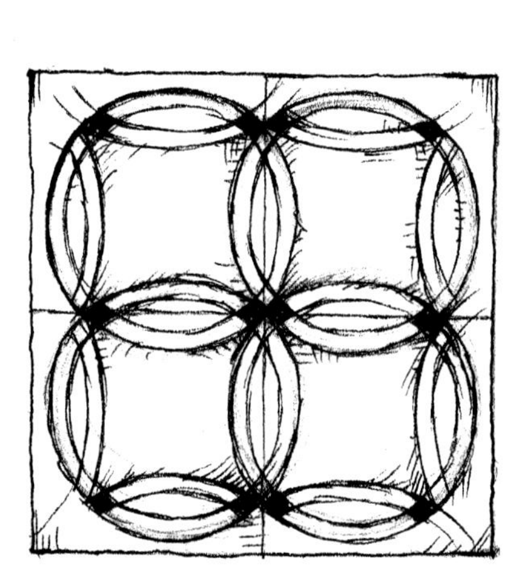

The Annunciation

And in the sixth month the angel Gabriel was sent from God unto a city of Galilee, named Nazareth, to a virgin espoused to a man whose name was Joseph, of the house of David; and the virgin's name was Mary.

And the angel came in unto her, and said, "Hail, thou that art highly favored, the Lord is with thee: blessed art thou among women."

And when she saw him, she was troubled at his saying, and cast in her mind what manner of salutation this should be.

And the angel said unto her,

"Fear not, Mary:
for thou hast found favor
with God."

"And, behold,
Thou shalt conceive in thy womb,
and bring forth a son,
and shalt call his name
Jesus
He shall be great, and shall be called
Son of the Highest
and of his kingdom
there shall be no end,
For with God
nothing is impossible."

And Mary said, "Behold the
handmaid of the Lord. Be it
unto me according to thy word."
And the angel departed.

nd

the Angel
of the Lord
appeared to Joseph
in a dream, saying
"Joseph,
thou Son of David,
~ Fear not ~
to take unto thee
Mary thy wife:
for that which is

conceived in her
is of the
Holy Spirit.”

Then Joseph
being raised
from sleep
did as the Angel
of the Lord
had bidden him
and took unto him
his wife.

The Visitation

And Mary arose in those days and
went into the hill country with haste,
into a city of Judah; and entered
into the house of Zechariah, and
greeted her cousin Elisabeth.
And it came to pass, that when
Elisabeth heard the salutation
of Mary, she was filled with
the Holy Spirit. And she
spoke out with a loud voice,
and said,
"Blessed art thou among women,
and blessed is the fruit of thy womb,
and blessed is she that Believed."

And Mary said,

eine Seele
erhebet den
Herrn. Und

my spirit hath rejoiced
in God my Savior.

For he hath regarded the low estate
of his handmaiden:
for, behold, from henceforth
all generations shall call me blessed.

For he that is mighty
hath done to me great things;
and holy is his name.

The Journey to Bethlehem

nd it came to pass in those days, that there went out a decree from Caesar Augustus, that all the world should be taxed.

And all went to be taxed, every one into his own city. And Joseph also went up from Galilee, out of the city of Nazareth, into Judea, unto the city of David, which is called Bethlehem; to be taxed with Mary his espoused wife, being great with child.

And so it was, that while they were there, the days were accomplished that she should be delivered.

And she brought forth her firstborn son, and wrapped him in swaddling clothes, and laid him in a manger; because there was no room for them in the inn.

And there were in the
same country shepherds
abiding in the field, keeping
watch over their flock by night.

And, lo,
the Angel of the Lord
came upon them,
and the glory of the Lord
shone round about them,
and they were afraid.

And the angel
said unto them,
Fear not
for, behold, I bring you
good tidings of great
joy, which shall be to
all people. For unto you
is born this day in the
city of David a Savior,
which is Christ the
Lord.

And this shall be
a sign unto you:
Ye shall find the
babe wrapped in
swaddling clothes,
lying in a manger.
And suddenly there was
with the angel a multitude of
the heavenly host, praising God,
And saying,

Glory to God
in the highest
and on earth peace
good will toward men.

Adoration

And the shepherds
said one to another,
"Let us now go even unto Bethlehem,
and see this thing which the Lord
hath made known unto us."
And they came with haste,
and found Mary, and Joseph,
and the babe lying in a manger.

The Presentation

When the days of Mary's purification according to the law of Moses were accomplished, they brought JESUS to Jerusalem to present him to the Lord.

And, behold, there was a man in Jerusalem whose name was Simeon. He was just and devout, and the Holy Spirit was upon him.

And it was revealed to him by the Holy Spirit that he should not see death before he had seen the ord's hrist.

And he came by the spirit into the temple when Mary and Joseph brought in the child

esus.

Simeon took the child up in his
arms, and blessed God, and said,

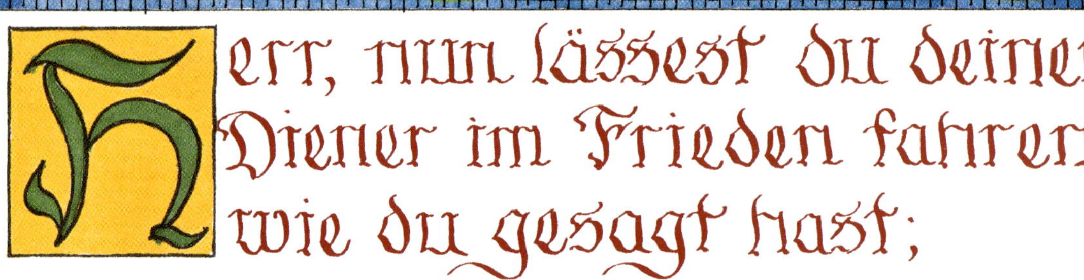

Herr, nun lässest du deinen
Diener im Frieden fahren,
wie du gesagt hast;

Lord, now lettest thou thy servant
depart in peace, according to thy word;

Denn meine Augen haben deinen
Heiland gesehen, welchen du
bereitet hast vor allen Völkern,
ein Licht zu erleuchten die Heiden,
und zum Preis deines Volks Israels.

For mine eyes have seen thy salvation
which thou hast prepared
before the face of all people,
a light to lighten the Gentiles,
and the glory of thy people Israel.

And there was Anna, a Prophetess, the daughter of Phanuel. She was of great age, a widow of many years, never departing from the temple, serving God with fastings and prayer night and day.
And she came in just at that moment and gave thanks likewise unto the Lord. And she spoke of the child to all them that looked for redemption in Jerusalem.
And Joseph and Mary marveled at those things that were spoken.

The Visit of the Magi

ow

when Jesus
was born in
Bethlehem of Judea
in the days of
Herod the king,

ehold,

there came wise men
from the east
to Jerusalem,

aying,

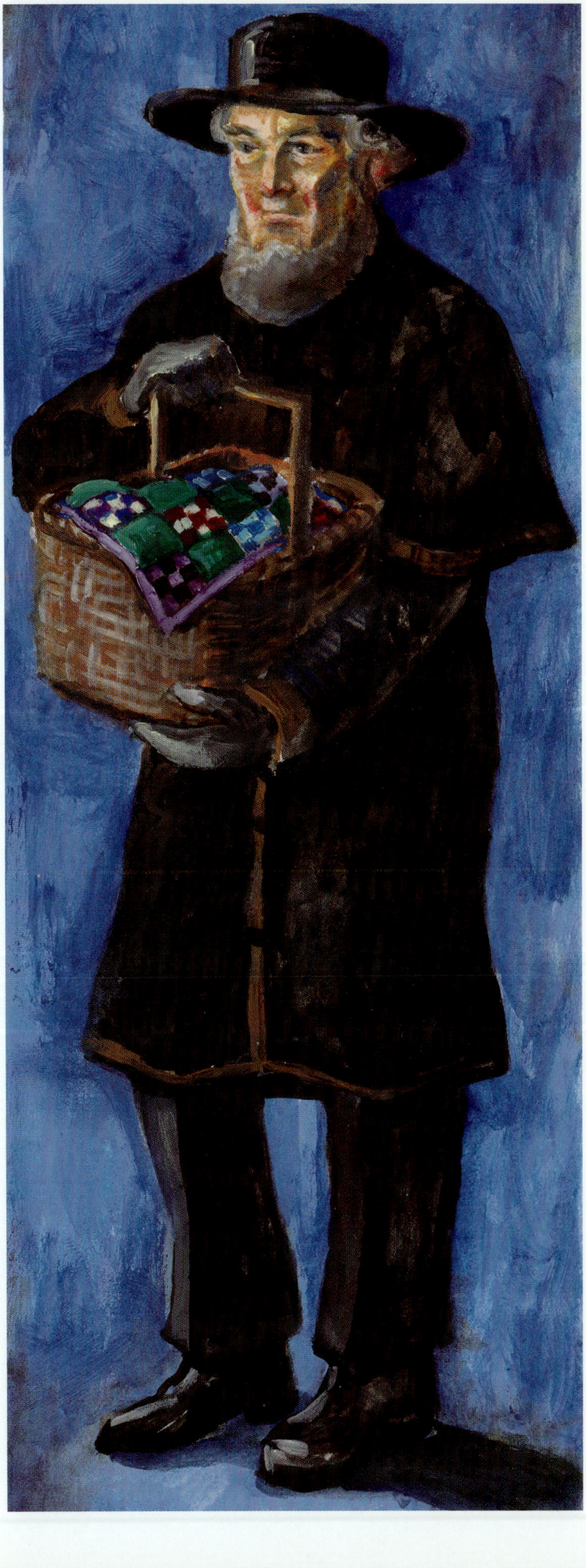

Where is he that is born King of the Jews? for we have seen His star in the east, and are come to worship Him.

And, lo, the star, which they saw in the east, went before them, till it came and stood over where the young child was.

When they saw the star, they rejoiced with exceeding great joy.

And when they were come into the house, they saw the young child with Mary his mother, and fell down, and worshiped him: and when they opened their treasures they presented unto Him gifts.

The Flight into Egypt

ehold, the Angel of the Lord
appeared to Joseph in a dream,
saying,

Arise
and take the young child
and his mother
and flee into Egypt,
and be thou there
until I bring thee word:
for Herod will seek the young child
to destroy him.

When Joseph arose, he took
the young child and his mother
by night, and departed into Egypt.

But
when Herod was dead,
behold,
an Angel of the Lord
appeared in a dream
to Joseph in Egypt,
saying,
Arise
and take
the young child
and his mother
and go into
the land of Israel:
for they are dead
which sought
the young child's
life.

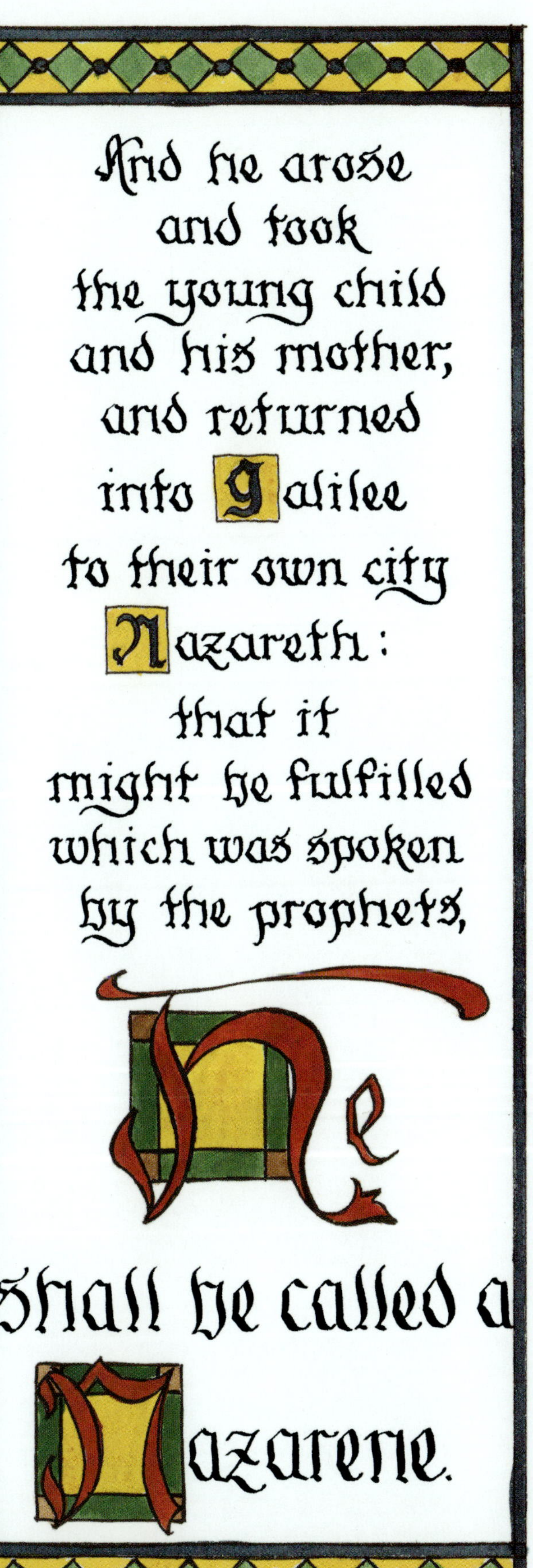
And he arose
and took
the young child
and his mother,
and returned
into Galilee
to their own city
Nazareth:
that it
might be fulfilled
which was spoken
by the prophets,
He
shall be called a
Nazarene.

For God so loved the world, that he gave his only begotten Son, that whosoever believeth in him should not perish, but have eternal life.
And the child grew,
and waxed strong in spirit,
filled with wisdom:
and the grace of God
was upon him.

And Mary
kept all these things
and pondered them
in her heart.

Guten Abend,
gute Nacht.